Awesome Fun Facts for Trivia Lovers

Mind-Blowing Facts about Your Body You Won't Believe

FACTHUB STUDIOS

FACTHUB STUDIO

Presents

Mind-Blowing Facts about Your Body You Won't Believe

1. Glitter in Your gut

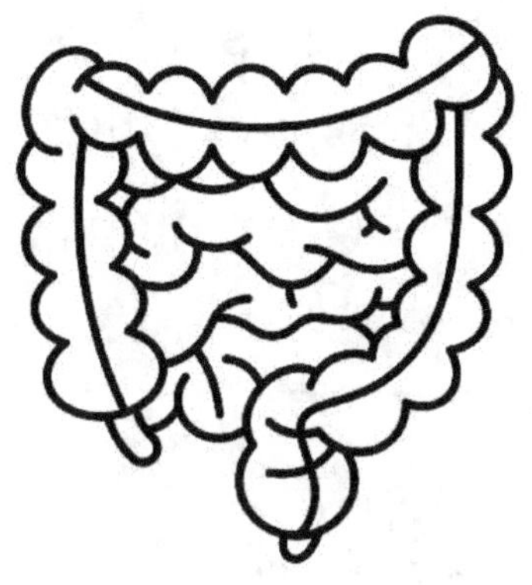

Imagine sprinkling edible glitter on your breakfast cereal, except it's already there, hidden in tiny, shimmery specks. That's the surprising truth about mica, a mineral found in some foods like baked goods, processed cheese, and even certain fruits. This microscopic glitter, far from adding glamour to your meal, simply hitches a ride through your digestive system, hanging out for months!

Don't worry, though, this sparkly stowaway is completely harmless. Mica's inert nature means it passes through your body undigested, leaving you with a touch of internal sparkle. Imagine a disco ball in your digestive tract, minus the dancing lights, of course. While it might seem strange, mica is actually a common food additive, used for its ability to give foods a pearlescent sheen.

So next time you bite into a slice of cake or sprinkle glitter on your craft project, remember your body and the world around you are filled with more hidden connections than you might think. And who knows, maybe that sparkly poop you flush away is actually a tiny testament to the surprising things we ingest every day!

2. Taste bud map

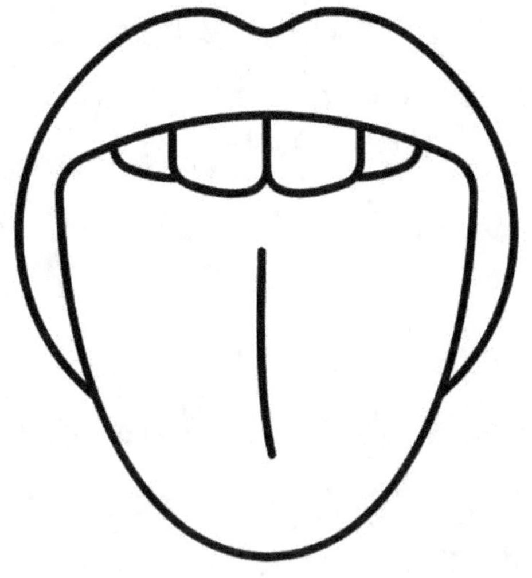

Forget the boring tongue map you saw in grade school the reality is way more delicious and complex!. Your tongue isn't just a taste bud blob it's a gourmet map with distinct districts craving different flavors. Picture a mini culinary world on your tongue

On the sunny tip, sugar reigns supreme. Sweet treats send this area into a dance of joy, amplifying the pleasure of every spoonful of ice cream or juicy berry. Just a bit further back, on the sides, the salty squad takes over. Craving chips or a sprinkle of ocean-kissed sea salt? These taste buds are your partners in savory crime.

But venture all the way to the back of your tongue, and you enter a whole other flavor dimension. This is where the bitter brigade resides, ready to tackle dark chocolate, strong coffee, or a leafy green salad. While some might shy away from this intense sensation, these taste buds offer a sophisticated appreciation for complex flavors and their hidden benefits?

So, the next time you savor a bite, remember you're not just enjoying a meal, you're embarking on a sensory expedition across your own personal tastebud map. Each lick, sip, and chew is a mini adventure, revealing the surprising diversity of your tongue's flavor preferences. It's time to ditch the outdated map and appreciate the real, dynamic landscape of taste that resides within you!

3. Super Senses

Forget the X-Men, there are real-life humans with superpowers right under our noses! Step aside, night vision and telekinesis, because the true marvels lie in our senses, sometimes amplified to extraordinary levels.

Imagine a world where every sunrise explodes into a billion unseen hues, where every raindrop whispers its acidity on your tongue. That's the reality for tetrachromats, individuals who possess four cone types in their eyes, granting them the ability to perceive 100 million more shades of color than the average human. Their vision is a kaleidoscope, where reds deepen into velvets and blues shimmer with hidden turquoise whispers.

And if seeing the unseen wasn't enough, meet the water whisperers. These individuals, gifted with hypertaste, can taste the subtle differences in water's mineral composition, turning them into human pH meters. Imagine taking a sip and discerning the limestone whispers of a mountain stream or the salty tang of the ocean every gulp a mini chemical symphony on your tongue.

These super senses are a testament to the extraordinary diversity of human biology. They remind us that our bodies are not fixed machines, but vessels capable of experiencing the world in ways we can only imagine. So the next time you bite into a strawberry or gaze at a sunset, remember someone out there might be tasting its hidden sweetness or witnessing its unseen spectrum of colors. The human body is a playground of potential, and who knows what other super senses await discovery!

4. Talking Stomach

Imagine a world where your stomach isn't just a silent grumbler demanding food, but a full-fledged conversationalist with a penchant for noisy gossip. That's the reality for those afflicted with "stomach rumbling syndrome," a condition that turns your gut into a chatty neighbor, broadcasting its every rumble and bubble, even when you're happily stuffed.

Forget awkward silences during dinner parties this syndrome ensures your digestive tract takes center stage, punctuating conversations with a series of gurgles, grumbles, and rumbles that would make a foghorn jealous. While hunger might trigger the occasional growl in the average tummy, this syndrome elevates the volume and frequency, transforming your internal orchestra into a cacophony of digestive pronouncements.

But don't worry, this noisy neighbor isn't a harbinger of doom. While embarrassing and occasionally inconvenient, stomach rumbling syndrome is a harmless condition, caused by involuntary contractions in the stomach muscles. It's like a mini earthquake happening within, churning and mixing your food with gusto, and sometimes, unfortunately, announcing its efforts to the world.

So next time your stomach decides to hold a press conference in the middle of your office meeting, remember it's not a sign of impending indigestion, but a quirk of your fascinatingly complex digestive system. Embrace the chatter, laugh it off, and maybe even give your gut a name for its lively personality. After all, a talking stomach is a surefire conversation starter, guaranteed to liven up any social gathering!

5. Mirror neurons

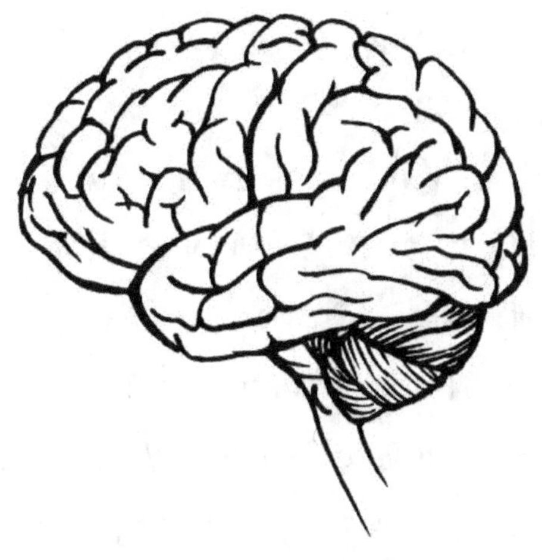

Ever catch yourself unconsciously mirroring someone's yawn or adjusting your posture after seeing them do the same? This isn't just a coincidence it's the magic of mirror neurons at work. These special brain cells are like social chameleons, firing not only when you perform an action but also when you observe someone else doing it. It's like having tiny empathy factories in your head, constantly building bridges of understanding between you and those around you.

Think of it as learning by osmosis. Watching someone tie their shoes or make a pancake activates the same neurons in your brain as if you were doing it yourself. This unconscious mirroring helps us grasp complex skills and behaviors through observation, accelerating our learning curve and fostering a sense of shared experience. It's why babies learn to smile and laugh by watching their parents, and why we instinctively feel awkward seeing someone stumble or grimace.

But mirror neurons do more than just copycat. They allow us to tune into the emotions and intentions of others. By feeling a reflection of what someone else is experiencing, we build empathy and social connection. Seeing someone cry triggers sadness in us, making us more likely to offer comfort. Witnessing someone's joy activates pleasure centers in our own brains, boosting our mood and strengthening the bond.

So the next time you catch yourself mirroring someone's actions, remember, it's more than just a quirky habit. It's a testament to the incredible power of our brains to connect, learn, and empathize through the invisible wires of shared experience. These hidden neurons are whispering bridges, weaving webs of understanding that make us human and help us navigate the beautiful chaos of social interaction.

6. Golden blood

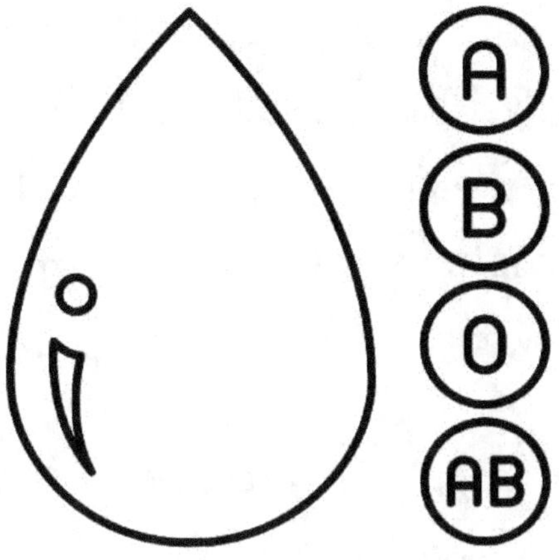

Imagine a blood type so precious, so unique, it could unlock life-saving transfusions for any person on Earth. Introducing Rhnull, the "golden blood" of the medical world, found in fewer than 50 individuals across the globe. This isn't just a rare type it's a revolution in compatibility.

Unlike other blood types, Rhnull lacks all the RhD protein antigens, the flags that trigger an immune response when mismatched blood enters the body. This makes it the universal donor, a key that fits every lock, a beacon of hope for patients with rare blood types who previously faced an agonizing wait for compatible transfusions. Rhnull is the lifeline for children with complex blood disorders, for accident victims in desperate need, and for those battling illnesses where every minute counts.

But the rarity of this golden blood comes with a heavy price. Finding an Rhnull donor is like searching for a needle in a haystack, a race against time and circumstance. Every known Rhnull donor becomes a vital link in a fragile chain, their blood a precious resource, carefully banked and monitored. They carry the weight of countless lives on their shoulders, knowing their unique gift can mean the difference between life and death for someone they may never meet.

So, the next time you think about blood types, remember this tale of the golden blood. Remember the individuals who carry this incredible gift and the hope they offer to those in desperate need. Rhnull is more than just a rare antigen it's a testament to the extraordinary diversity of human biology and the potential for one person to touch countless lives through sheer genetic uniqueness. The search for more Rhnull donors continues, a quest to unlock the potential of this golden blood and ensure that everyone, no matter how rare their type, has a fighting chance at life.

7. Hibernating humans

Forget bears and bats, there's a hibernator lurking closer than you think it's you! While the idea of humans taking a winter nap might sound like science fiction, a chilling case from Canada proved otherwise. In the throes of a blizzard, a woman's body temperature plummeted to a bone-chilling 89F, her breathing slowed to a whisper, and her pulse barely registered. She was, quite literally, in human hibernation.

This wasn't just a case of extreme sleepiness. Her brainwaves mirrored those of hibernating animals, and her metabolism slowed to a crawl, burning calories at a snail's pace. She slept for days, her body a silent, frigid fortress against the raging storm outside. When she finally emerged, blinking at the sun-drenched world, she was completely healthy, leaving scientists scratching their heads and rewriting the textbooks on human physiology.

While this case is unique, it opens a tantalizing window into the hidden potential of the human body. Could this be a vestigial trait, a forgotten echo of our ancient ancestors who weathered harsh winters in a similar state? Or is it a rare mutation, a biological quirk that allows some individuals to tap into an extreme energy—saving mode?

The possibilities are intriguing. Imagine astronauts hibernating on long journeys to distant planets, or injured patients entering a safe, metabolic hibernation to conserve resources and promote healing. While we're not about to trade our cozy beds for ice caves, the story of the hibernating human reminds us that our bodies are more than just flesh and bone they're vaults of hidden potential, waiting to be unlocked. Who knows, maybe the next time a snowstorm blankets the world, we'll all be taking a page out of this hibernator's book, curling up and letting our bodies take a magical, icy nap.

8. Fire resistance

Imagine staring into an inferno, flames licking at your skin, yet walking away seemingly untouched. Sounds like superhero territory, right? But for a few incredibly rare individuals, this firewalking feat isn't fiction, it's reality. These lucky souls possess a hidden superpower temporary fire resistance triggered by the body's own chemistry.

While the science behind it isn't fully understood, the adrenaline surge in extreme situations is likely the key. This surge can raise your pain threshold, numb nerve endings, and even alter skin chemistry, potentially turning it into a temporary fire shield. Imagine your skin momentarily morphing into a heat-resistant barrier, deflecting flames and protecting you from scorching temperatures.

But don't mistake this rare quirk for an invitation to play with fire. The level and duration of this resistance varies dramatically, and even for these fire-kissed individuals, prolonged exposure can still cause severe burns. Think of it as a safety net, not an invincible cloak.

These real-life firewalkers remind us of the incredible, and often unpredictable, ways our bodies can adapt and respond to danger. They are living testaments to the hidden potential within us, the hidden superpowers waiting to be unlocked in the face of extraordinary circumstances. So next time you hear a fire alarm, remember, even in the fiercest flames, there may be a spark of resilience, a hidden ember of human potential waiting to be ignited.

9. Echolocation humans

Forget sonar and fancy gadgets, some humans navigate the world with a sound all their own clicking tongues and weaving echoes into a 3D map of their surroundings. These remarkable individuals, often those who are blind, have mastered the art of echolocation, transforming ordinary sounds into a superpower that helps them navigate with astonishing precision.

Imagine snapping your fingers, not just for rhythm, but to paint the world in sound. Each click bounces off walls, furniture, even people, creating a symphony of echoes that sing a detailed song of their location. Blinding darkness becomes a canvas of reflected sound, where a sharp echo translates to a nearby wall, a softer chime whispers of a distant doorway, and the rustling of leaves paints a picture of a passing breeze.

But mastering this sonic superpower takes dedication and practice. Years of honing their listening skills allow these echolocators to decipher the subtle nuances of each echo, like a seasoned musician interpreting a complex melody. They learn to gauge the distance, size, and even texture of objects with an accuracy that rivals sonar technology. Imagine walking through a crowded market, not with your eyes, but with your ears, identifying stalls, dodging people, and finding your way with an uncanny precision born from clicks and echoes.

The story of echolocating humans is a testament to the remarkable adaptability of the brain and the incredible potential hidden within our senses. It's a reminder that even in the absence of sight, the world can be painted in sound, a mesmerizing landscape waiting to be explored with a tongue as a paintbrush and echoes as the vibrant strokes.

10. Leaky gut

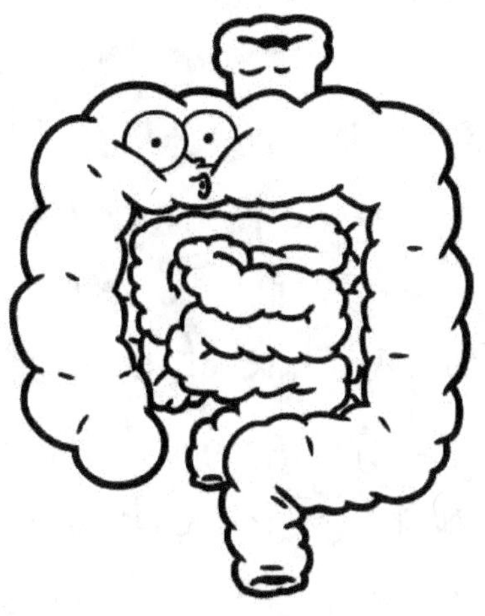

Ever feel like your stomach's holding a secret meeting of rebellious gas bubbles? Turns out, that gassy grumble might be whispering a bigger story the story of a leaky gut. Imagine your intestines, usually a tightly sealed fortress protecting your body from unwanted invaders, developing tiny cracks. Through these ''leaks,'' rogue food particles and nasty toxins sneak into your bloodstream, triggering a chain reaction of digestive distress and potentially setting the stage for chronic health problems.

This isn't just a tummy-ache tale. Leaky gut, also known as increased intestinal permeability, has been linked to a surprising range of ailments, from chronic fatigue and skin woes to allergies and even autoimmune diseases. Think of it as a tiny betrayal within, your loyal gut guard letting the bad guys slip through, causing internal chaos and confusion.
But don't panic! Leaky gut isn't a guaranteed one-way ticket to illness. It's often a contributing factor, a piece of the puzzle, rather than the entire picture. And the good news? There are ways to mend the leaks and tighten up your intestinal fortress. Dietary changes, stress management, and gut-friendly probiotics can all work towards patching up the cracks and restoring your gut's natural defenses.

So, the next time you feel that familiar gas bubble rumble, remember it might be a message from your gut. Listen closely, for it could be whispering about more than just indigestion. It could be a call to action, a reminder to nourish your inner ecosystem and rebuild the wall that protects your health. After all, a happy gut is a healthy you, and sometimes, all it takes is a little TLC to turn those gas bubbles into whispers of well-being.

11. Laughing gas Syndrome

Forget the awkward chuckle that gets stuck in your throat picture a world where laughter erupts like a volcanic eruption, seizing your body and refusing to let go. This is the bizarre reality of gelastic cataplexy, a neurological disorder where strong emotions, from surprise to joy, can trigger uncontrollable and prolonged fits of laughter. Imagine bursting into a giggle fit at a funeral, or erupting in uncontrollable guffaws during a tense exam that's the unpredictable rollercoaster ride of gelastic cataplexy.

But this isn't just a case of inappropriate giggles. The laughter itself can be overwhelming, leaving individuals gasping for air, struggling to speak, and even losing control of their limbs. It's like a rogue wave of amusement crashing over your nervous system, leaving you helpless and bewildered in its wake.

While the cause of gelastic cataplexy isn't fully understood, it's thought to be linked to an abnormal connection between the brain's emotional and motor centers. Strong emotions trigger a misfiring in the system, turning your laughter reflex from a gentle chuckle into a runaway train. Think of it as a faulty switch, throwing your emotions into a hyperdrive that leaves you helplessly giggling in the middle of a serious situation.

Despite its bizarre nature, gelastic cataplexy can be managed. Medication and therapy can help individuals regain control of their laughter and navigate the emotional minefield that triggers their involuntary giggles. And while the condition can be frustrating and isolating, it's also a reminder of the incredible complexity and fragility of the human brain, and the unexpected ways it can express emotions, even the joyful ones, in the most unexpected ways. So next time you hear someone laughing uncontrollably, remember, it might be more than just a funny joke it could be a whisper of the hidden wiring within our brains, where laughter and tears can dance a strange, unpredictable tango.

12. Rainbow blood

Imagine peering into a vial of human blood, expecting the familiar crimson, but instead encountering a vibrant emerald or a breathtaking amethyst hue. This isn't a sci-fi special effect it's the reality for some incredibly rare individuals who possess "rainbow blood." These mutations rewrite the script of human physiology, replacing the usual red hemoglobin with other pigments, transforming their blood into a living rainbow.

One such mutation replaces red hemoglobin with methemoglobin, a molecule with a distinctive green color. This rare condition, called methemoglobinemia, can arise from genetic mutations or even exposure to certain chemicals. Imagine looking in the mirror after a cut and seeing emerald droplets trickling down, a surreal beauty tinged with the potential dangers of oxygen deprivation.

Another mutation, sulfhemoglobinemia, replaces hemoglobin with sulfhemoglobin, a molecule that lends blood a deep purple hue. This condition, even rarer than methemoglobinemia, can be triggered by certain medications or even chronic sulfur exposure. Imagine the shock of seeing a bruise bloom not in shades of blue and yellow, but in a mesmerizing amethyst, a reminder that beneath our skin lies a kaleidoscope of hidden possibilities.

While these rainbow—hued individuals face challenges related to oxygen transport and potential health complications, their unique blood serves as a stunning testament to the diversity of human biology. It's a whispered secret within our veins, a reminder that the human body, even in its most basic functions, holds the potential for breathtaking beauty and unexpected twists on the expected. So next time you think about blood, remember, it might not always be the familiar red Sometimes, it can be a canvas for the most unexpected colors, whispering stories of hidden mutations and the endless wonder of the human form.

13. Super Saliva

Imagine a world where your spit bubbles aren't mere whispers, but geysers erupting from your mouth. Meet the queen of drool, a young girl who holds the record for most saliva produced in five minutes a jaw-dropping 1 liter! This isn't just a case of forgetting to swallow your gum it's a story of Super Saliva, a bizarre twist on a basic bodily function.

Scientists suspect a nerve anomaly might be behind this impressive flow. Imagine a rogue wire in the salivary system, amplifying the usual trickle into a torrential downpour. It's like turning the "spit" knob on your body to max, transforming your mouth into a mini Niagara Falls.

While this super saliva might seem like a messy superpower, it comes with challenges. Imagine constantly battling overflowing glands, feeling like a leaky faucet with no off switch. It's a symphony of sloshing sounds, soggy shirts, and a perpetual need for tissues. But here's the unexpected twist this girl's unique talent has been used for research, helping scientists understand the mechanisms of salivary production and its role in oral health.

So next time you reach for a mint after lunch, remember the queen of drool and her super saliva. She's a testament to the incredible diversity of the human body, a reminder that even the most mundane functions can hold hidden potential, bizarre quirks, and the chance to rewrite the rules of what we think is normal. And who knows, maybe one day, super saliva will be recognized as a superpower after all, not just a messy marvel of human biology.

14. Human Slime

Forget gooey puddles and creepy crawlies, the real human slime is happening inside you right now! Imagine your entire respiratory system lined with a sticky, gooey barrier, not for gross-out factor, but for heroic defense. This slimy shield, known as mucus, is your unsung hero, the silent guardian standing between you and every nasty invader lurking in the air.

Think of it as a microscopic flypaper, catching dust, pollen, and even tiny critters before they can wreak havoc in your lungs. Tiny hairs called cilia act like rowdy bouncers, constantly waving and pushing this sticky goo, sweeping away the unwanted guests and keeping your airways clean. It's a messy, gooey operation, but it's crucial for keeping your lungs healthy and happy.

And don't be fooled by its snotty reputation! This human slime is actually a complex cocktail of proteins, sugars, and electrolytes, each playing a vital role in its protective mission. It traps moisture, preventing your lungs from drying out, and even contains antimicrobial defenses, like tiny ninja warriors, ready to fight off any invading bacteria.

So next time you reach for a tissue, remember the humble human slime. It's a gooey testament to the body's ingenuity, a silent guardian working tirelessly to keep you healthy, breath after breath. Give it a silent cheer, the unsung hero of your respiratory system, the champion of clean air, the king or queen of the human slime!

15. Phantom limb

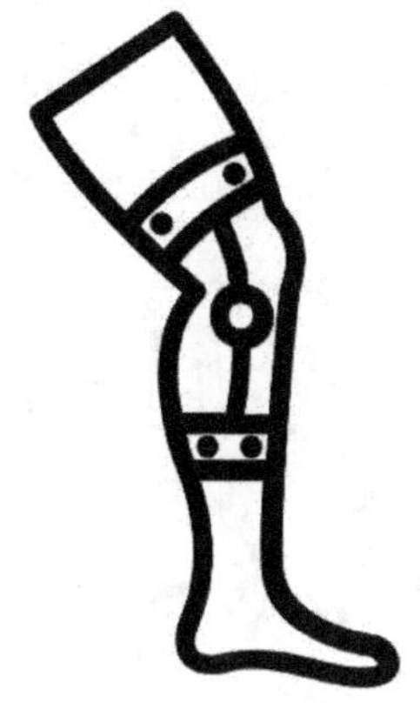

Imagine a phantom itch scratching a limb you no longer have, or a phantom breeze tingling fingers that have vanished. This isn't a ghost story, but the reality of phantom limb pain, a bizarre sensation experienced by many amputees. Even with their limb gone, their brain still maps sensations onto its phantom location, creating a ghostly echo of what once was.

Why does this happen? It's all about rewiring. After amputation, the brain regions responsible for the lost limb don't simply shut down. Instead, they get repurposed, taking on new functions or merging with neighboring areas. This rewiring can sometimes lead to misfiring signals, creating the illusion of sensations in the missing limb. It's like a map with a city erased, but the roads still leading there, phantom paths to a place that's no more.

Phantom limb pain can be a complex and challenging experience. The sensations can range from tingling and itching to burning and crushing pain. Some even report feeling the missing limb move or change position. While the pain can be debilitating, it's important to remember that it's not happening in the missing limb itself, but in the brain. With proper treatment, including therapy and medication, many amputees learn to manage and even overcome this phantom pain, allowing them to reclaim a sense of wholeness and move forward.

So next time you see someone with an amputated limb, remember the possibility of phantom sensations dancing in the air. It's a reminder of the incredible plasticity of the brain, its ability to adapt and even create its own reality, even in the face of loss. And while the experience might be eerie, it's also a testament to the enduring connection between mind and body, a whisper of the limb that once was, echoing in the vast landscapes of the brain.

16. Sleeping Beauty Syndrome

Forget fairy tales the real Sleeping Beauty story is far stranger than fiction. Imagine not just falling asleep, but disappearing into a slumber so deep, so impenetrable, it steals weeks of your life. Meet the woman afflicted with Kleine-Levin Syndrome, a rare condition that cast her into a living Sleeping Beauty cycle, trapping her in a world of profound sleep for days, even weeks at a time.

This wasn't just catching some extra ZZZ's. Her sleep was a fortress, impenetrable by even the loudest alarms or most persistent prodding. Her world shrunk to a dim, barely conscious state, where even basic functions like eating and speaking became monumental tasks. Tube feeding replaced meals, and days blurred into nights, stolen by this mysterious slumber.

But unlike the fairytale princess, there was no spindle prick or handsome prince to break the spell. The cause of Kleine-Levin is shrouded in mystery, possibly linked to immune system glitches or abnormalities in the brain's sleep-wake circuitry. It's a cruel twist of fate, transforming sleep, usually a restorative balm, into a thief of time and life.

While there's no magic kiss to awaken these real-life sleeping Beauties, hope glimmers in the form of medication and therapies that can manage symptoms and shorten the episodes. Each awakening, however rare, is a victory, a precious window back to the world stolen by sleep. So, the next time you snuggle into bed, remember this sleeping beauty's story. It's a reminder of the body's hidden mysteries, the fragility of consciousness, and the precious gift of wakefulness, a time to cherish every minute, every sunrise, every moment stolen back from the clutches of a slumber that is anything but a fairytale dream.

17. The Bionic Man

Imagine a world where missing limbs aren't the end, but the beginning of a new chapter. In 1966, that world became reality for a man named Peter Bowman, the recipient of the world's first successful artificial arm implant. This wasn't just a clunky prosthetic it was a marvel of engineering, a fusion of acrylic and steel that offered a glimpse into the future of bionic limbs.

Bowman's original arm was lost in a motorcycle accident, leaving him facing a life of limitations. But with this pioneering surgery, he regained some semblance of control. The artificial limb, though stiff and lacking fine motor skills, allowed him to perform basic tasks, from gripping objects to feeding himself. It wasn't a full restoration, but it was a giant leap, a testament to the ingenuity of human medicine and the relentless pursuit of overcoming limitations.

Bowman's story became a beacon of hope for countless amputees. His bionic arm, though primitive compared to today's sophisticated prosthetics, paved the way for advancements in materials, technology, and neural integration. Each new generation of bionic limbs owes a debt to Bowman, his willingness to be a pioneer and his courage to embrace a future where technology could bridge the gap between loss and possibility.

So, the next time you see someone with a prosthetic limb, remember Peter Bowman, the Bionic Man who dared to dream of a world where missing limbs wouldn't mean missing out on life. He is a symbol of human resilience, of the unwavering spirit that pushes the boundaries of what's possible, and of the incredible journey we're on towards a future where bionic limbs are not just tools, but extensions of ourselves, seamlessly blending technology and humanity to rewrite the narrative of loss and limitation.

18. Singing bones

Imagine a world where your body isn't just a vessel for music, it is music itself. A world where tapping on your shinbone produces a delicate chime, a gentle melody whispered by your ribcage with every breath. This isn't some fantastical dream it's the bizarre reality of musical bone disease, a condition that turns your skeleton into a living, resonant instrument.

This isn't just about a few creaky joints. Musical bone disease, also known as Paget's disease of bone, alters the structure of your bones, making them abnormally dense and brittle. But amidst this fragility lies a hidden musicality. The altered bone structure acts as a sounding board, amplifying vibrations and transforming them into audible tones. A tap on your arm becomes a plucked string, a brush against your ribs a haunting xylophone melody.

This unexpected symphony can be a source of wonder and amusement. Imagine playing your own body like a percussion instrument, your fingers tapping out rhythms on your chest, your feet drumming a beat against your knees. But the music can also be disconcerting. Unexpected bumps or jostles can trigger a jarring cacophony, turning a simple walk into a bone-rattling concerto.

Yet, even in its strangeness, musical bone disease offers a unique perspective on the human body. It reminds us that our bones, often seen as rigid and static, are living, dynamic structures, constantly adapting and resonating to the world around us. It's a tangible reminder that the human body is a complex symphony of processes, where even the seemingly silent bones can sing their own hidden song.

So, next time you hear someone tapping their foot or drumming their fingers, remember the whispers of music within us all. Remember the possibility that beneath our skin, beneath our flesh, lies a hidden orchestra, waiting to be played, waiting to remind us that even the most unexpected parts of us can resonate with the beauty and complexity of life.

And who knows, maybe one day, musical bone disease won't just be a medical anomaly, but a celebrated art form. Imagine concerts where virtuoso bone musicians perform, their bodies transformed into instruments, their melodies echoing the intricate rhythms of the human experience. Perhaps then, the whispers of our singing bones will become a powerful chorus, a testament to the boundless possibilities hidden within the human form.

19. Your own echo

Ever belted out a shower tune, only to be startled by your own amplified echo bouncing off the tiles? Well, it's not just the steamy acoustics creating a mini concert in your bathroom. Turns out, your skull's in on the act too, playing a secret instrument your voice!

Imagine this as you sing, your vocal cords vibrate, sending sound waves outward. But here's the twist these waves don't just travel into the air they also travel through your jawbone and into your skull. This bone conduction creates a second sound wave, vibrating the tiny bones in your inner ear just like the original wave did. Suddenly, you're hearing your own voice twice once through the air, and once through the whisper of your vibrating skull.

This eerie dual-track phenomenon creates a slightly delayed echo, giving your shower tunes a touch of otherworldly resonance. It's like having a built-in sound system in your head, a mini concert hall amplifying your voice with the subtle tremor of your own bones. So, next time you serenade the shampoo bottles, remember, it's not just the acoustics your skull's joining in the chorus, a silent partner in your bathroom symphony, adding a touch of bone-borne magic to your vocal performance.

But this skull-conducted echo isn't just a shower quirk. It's a fascinating reminder of how interconnected our senses are. It shows how a single sound wave can travel through different avenues, reaching our ears in multiple ways, each adding its own subtle nuance to the listening experience. So, the next time you hear an echo, close your eyes and listen closely. You might just hear the whisper of your own bones, singing along in the hidden chambers of your skull.

20. Brainwaves control robots

Imagine a world where your thoughts aren't just silent whispers in your head, but potent commands that bend the world to your will. This isn't science fiction it's the burgeoning reality of brain-computer interfaces BCIS, where your brainwaves dance with technology, allowing you to control robots with the mere flick of your mind.

Gone are the clunky joysticks and buttons. With BCIs, you simply think about moving your hand, and a robotic appendage mirrors your intent with uncanny precision. Imagine a paraplegic willing their steps, their thoughts translating into leg movements that propel a robotic exoskeleton. Imagine a surgeon guiding a scalpel with the deftness of their mind, their neural commands weaving through wires to control a robotic arm with millimetric accuracy.

But the future isn't just about mimicking limbs. Picture a world where your thoughts control drones soaring through the sky, robots navigating hazardous environments, or even simple devices responding to your mental commands. Imagine flipping channels with a thought, silencing an alarm with a mental sigh, or even controlling the temperature in your room with a mere flicker of your mind's thermostat.

While this mind-melding technology is still in its infancy, the possibilities are mind-boggling. It holds the promise of restoring independence to those with disabilities, revolutionizing surgery, and even blurring the lines between human and machine. So next time you close your eyes and imagine yourself moving something with your mind, remember, it's not just a daydream it's a glimpse into a future where our thoughts are no longer confined within our skulls, but unleashed onto the world, shaping and controlling the robots that dance to the silent symphony of our brainwaves.